YOU MIGHT BE FROM NOVA SCOTIA IF...

Michael de Adder

MacIntyre Purcell Publishing Inc.

MacIntyre Purcell Publishing Inc.
194 Hospital Rd.
Lunenburg, Nova Scotia
B0J 2C0
(902) 640-3350

www.macintyrepurcell.com
info@macintyrepurcell.com

Printed and bound in Canada by Friesens

ISBN: 978-1-77276-133-7

Library and Archives Canada Cataloguing in Publication Title: You might still be from Nova Scotia if... / Michael de Adder. Names: De Adder, Michael, 1967- author. Identifiers: Canadiana 20190112638 | ISBN 9781772761337 (softcover) Subjects: LCSH: Nova Scotia—Social life and customs—Caricatures and cartoons. | LCSH: Canadian wit and humor, Pictorial. | LCGFT: Comics (Graphic works) Classification: LCC FC2311.3 .D43 2019 | DDC 971.6—dc23

MacIntyre Purcell Publishing Inc. would like to acknowledge the financial support of the Government of Canada and the Nova Scotia Department of Tourism, Culture and Heritage.

FOR JIM

FOREWORD

… well, if you knew in May 2019 that Michael de Adder was a lethally-brilliant cartoonist — an exquisite draftsman and a deadly observer who eviscerates the pompous and the hypocritical as fast as a cat can swat a bubble.

A month later, of course, the whole world learned about de Adder's penchant for hurling the devastating truth at power, when he published his viral cartoon of Donald Trump standing beside a golf cart looking down on the drowned bodies of Óscar Alberto Martínez Ramírez and his two-year-old daughter, and asking the victims, "Mind if I play through?" There it is, in a blinding flash: the aloof callousness of Trump's attitude towards other human beings, particularly the desperate and the needy. Not surprisingly, the cartoon quickly blazed its way around the world.

And for doing his job superbly, of course, Mike de Adder was fired. His employers, the billionaire Irving family — who own all the newspapers in New Brunswick, and do a lot of business in the US — made it clear that there was no connection between the cartoon and the dismissal. Oh, no. Perish the thought.

However, you might still be from Nova Scotia if the dominant newspaper in your province *did* publish the Trump cartoon. Kudos to the *Chronicle Herald*.

Anyway, the whole world now knows that Michael de Adder is a splendid example of the way a sense of humour expresses and fortifies a commitment to radical sanity, a sense of intellectual and political balance. What the rest of the world does not know is de Adder's tender side — and that's what this book captures.

This book is a love letter to Nova Scotia aimed directly at Nova Scotians. These are images of what we know and love, quirky enthusiasms that we share. The world's highest tides and biggest fiddle, the daffy dedication to donairs, the silliness of celebrating your location on an imaginary line marking the midway point between the Equator and the North Pole, Frankie MacDonald's lusty weather predictions, the argument over whether the world's best fish and chips are at John's Lunch in Dartmouth — or not.

We have the Cookie Monster — and also Cookie Rankin. If you don't know who Cookie Rankin is, you might <u>not</u> be from Nova Scotia after all. In that case, you might be tempted to wander down onto the black rocks at Peggy's Cove. Don't. Just don't.

If all this sounds terribly mysterious, turn to the notes at the back of the book, where All Is Revealed. If you <u>are</u> from Nova Scotia, and you've reached those last pages by reading the book, you'll probably have laughed out loud more than once — but you'll also have felt a poignant, wry amusement. This is who we are. And aren't we lucky to have such a splendid artist to show us to ourselves?

— Silver Donald Cameron

INTRODUCTION

When you have a bestselling book, there is a temptation to write a sequel right away. I didn't. I thought I said everything in the first book.

But as I travelled the province for the next few years, I kept seeing things I missed. The stuff that makes us unique surrounds us every day.

Whether I was in Bridgewater or Lunenburg in the summer, or taking my kids to soccer or ringette in Berwick or Cape Breton, visiting family in New Glasgow or Kentville, I kept getting inspired by things I saw or people I met. I slowly started accumulating another book.

Like the first book, this book is less about places and more about people, the people of Nova Scotia.

I didn't want to fall back on stereotypes. Writing a book of stereotypes is easy. Capturing the common experiences of a diverse population is hard. We are not a province just of fishermen and longshoremen anymore, despite what our tourism advertisements might portray. We are a modern society with modern problems that still has a close connection to the sea. And, more importantly, we have close connections to each other.

• • •

A lot of people helped me with this book.

Meredith MacKinlay has been the most help on all my books. She's part angry English teacher and part motivational coach. She uses big words like *apostrophe* and *ellipsis*, while I use "air comma" and "dot-dot-dot." She's always reasonable when I ask her to do something in an unreasonable time period.

When I started this book, I started a chat group with Stephen Bornais, David Rodenhiser, Shaune MacKinlay and Beth Johnston, all are former journalists who worked with me at one time. Just listening to them chat about growing up in Nova Scotia inspired specific cartoons and influenced many others. Either one of them could have written their own Nova Scotia book. Good thing that none of them can draw. Suckers!

The Hemlock group formed another sounding board for ideas — Greg Little, Shaune MacKinlay (same as above), and Joanne and Julian Marchant were helpful with ideas and pointed out a few misses.

Todd Battis, a friend for most of my life, and one of the funniest people I know, came up with suggestions, tweaks and reminded me of things like chase the ace and other stories he's covered for CTV.

Bob Murphy only made one suggestion, and I turned it into two cartoons (Page 20 and 21) and thank you to Cathy from New Glasgow for page 44.

My Caper friends from Mount Allison University, Irene MacKinnon, MaryJane MacDonald and Laurie MacInnis, made sure all Cape Breton cartoons were accurate. And gave me endless encouragement.

Other people I couldn't have done without were cousins Kathy Barrie, Lori and Mark MacDonald, Erin Dwyer King (also a person who could write her own book) and Natalie Dwyer-Edinger.

My brothers Paul and David De Adder were of no help, as usual. (Like on a scale of one to ten: a complete zero.) BUT they gave me moral support when I needed it and were there for me no matter what time of day. They aren't just brothers, they are my best friends. In the middle of the book, Paul (David would have done the same) gave up a week of vacation to help me when all hell broke loose. I will forever be in his debt.

I would like to say a special thank you to the extended Coneen family and friends.

And I'd like to thank Gail, my wife, for doing all the driving, soccer, ringette, groceries, driving and more driving — did I mention driving? — when I had to work on this book. And thanks to my daughters Meaghan and Bridget for understanding and being thoughtful young people. I can do more of the driving now. (True story: before I even finished the previous sentence, I got asked to drive Meaghan to meet her friends.) I love you all.

— Michael de Adder

YOU MIGHT *STILL* BE FROM NOVA SCOTIA IF...

YOU ARE OFTEN REMINDED THAT WE ARE ALL FAMILY.

IT'S NOT THE HEAT, IT'S THE HUMIDITY.

IT'S EASY TO SPOT THE COME-FROM-AWAYS
AT PEGGY'S COVE.

YOU ARRIVE JUST AS THE FERRY IS CANCELLED.

TAKING A VACATION DURING MARCH BREAK IS A ROLL OF THE DICE.

YOU SEARCHED EVERYWHERE FOR $4.

A SIGN TELLS YOU TO EXPECT WINTER CONDITIONS AND IT'S AUGUST.

YOU THINK NOVA SCOTIANS COULD FORM ONE OF THE BEST FORWARD LINES IN HOCKEY.

YOU KNOW ONE OF THE GREATEST DEFENCEMEN
OF ALL TIME WAS FROM INVERNESS.

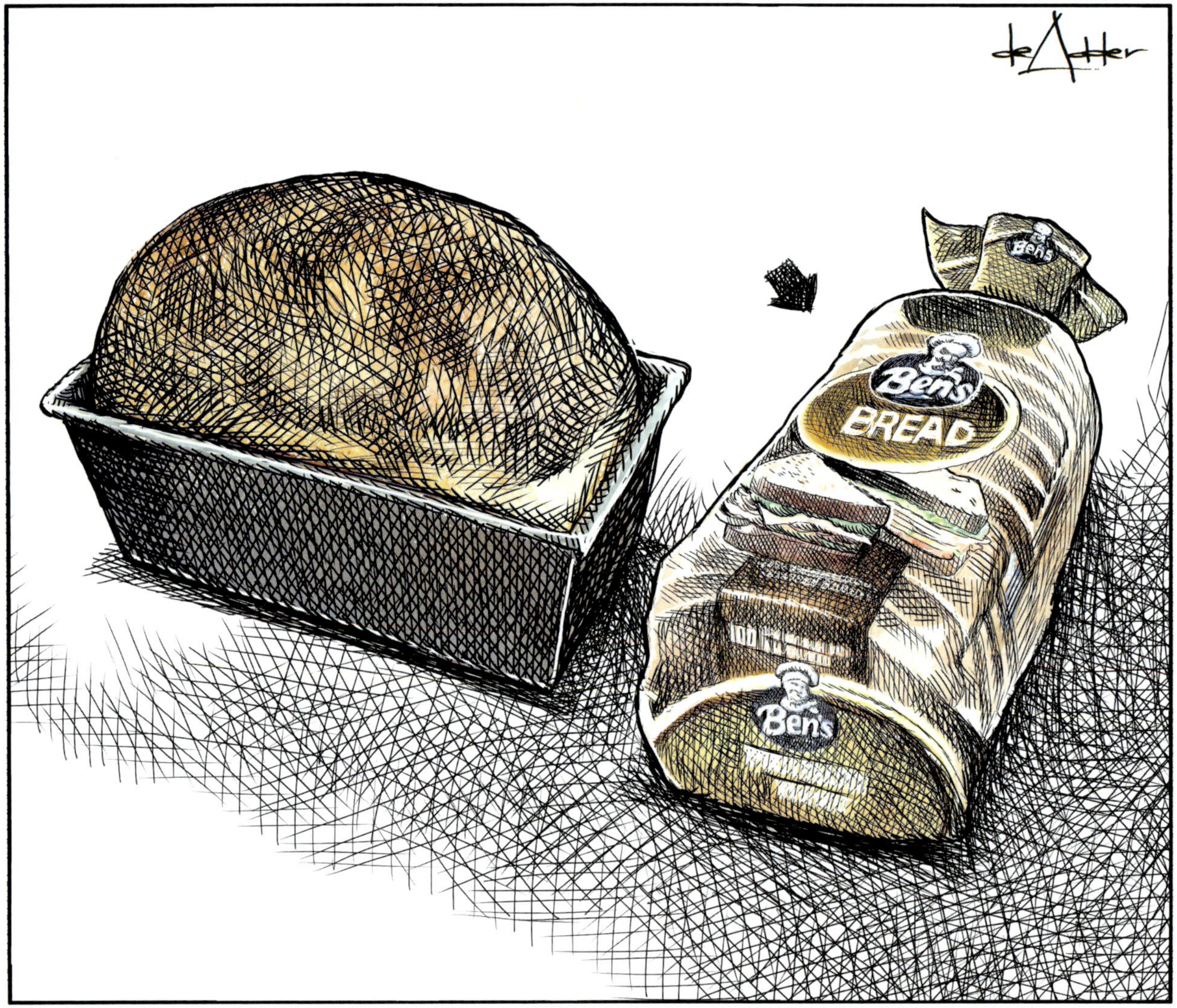

YOU CALL THIS BOUGHTEN BREAD.

THE SMELL OF WARM BREAD REMINDS YOU OF HOME.

BEFORE SEPTEMBER 29, 2003 YOU DIDN'T TAKE HURRICANE WARNINGS SERIOUSLY.

AFTER SEPTEMBER 29, 2003 YOU TOOK HURRICANE WARNINGS SERIOUSLY.

IT SNOWS IN HALIFAX... AND THE POWER GOES OUT IN HALIFAX.

IT SNOWS IN SYDNEY... AND THE POWER GOES OUT IN HALIFAX.

YOU CELEBRATED THE DAY IKEA CAME BACK TO HALIFAX.

YOU CURSED THE DAY IKEA CAME BACK TO HALIFAX.

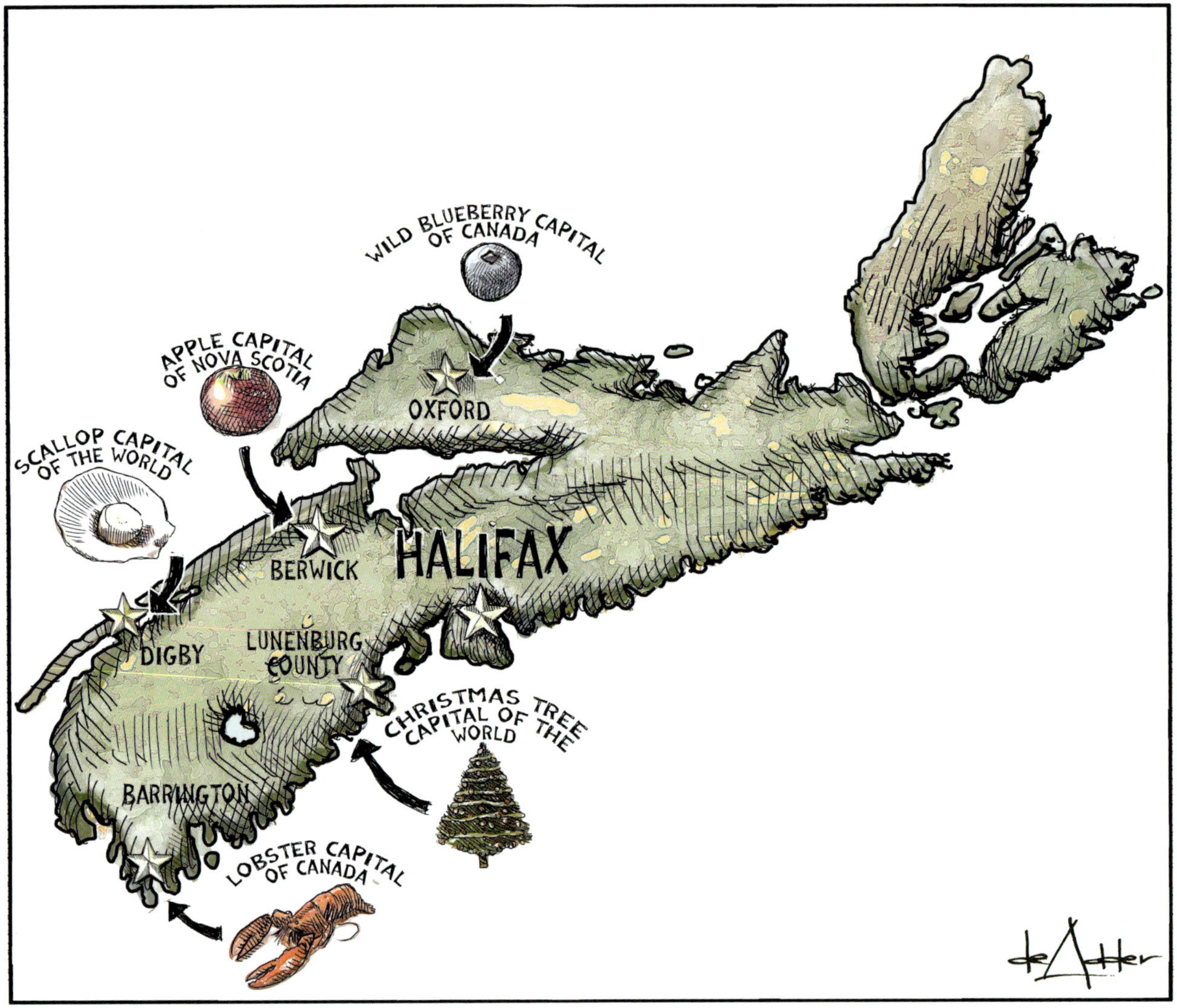

YOU KNOW NOVA SCOTIA HAS MORE THAN ONE CAPITAL.

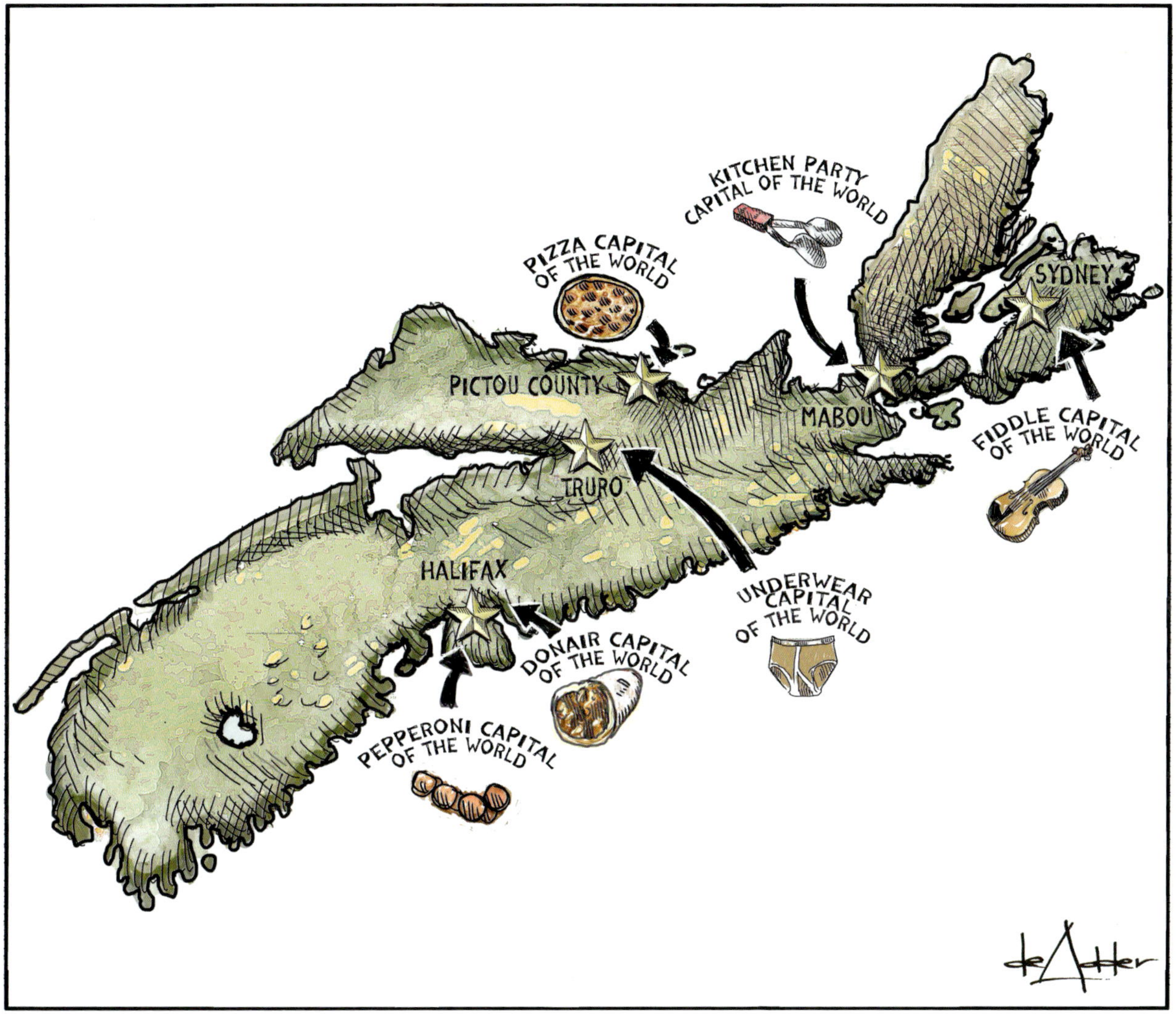

YOU THINK NOVA SCOTIA COULD HAVE EVEN MORE CAPITALS.

YOU NEVER ORDER LOBSTER IN A RESTAURANT.

YOU KNOW SOMEBODY WHO KNOWS SOMEBODY WHO CAN GET LOBSTERS CHEAP.

YOU'VE BEEN CALLED A SOOK.

THE WORD "PUCK" IS A VERB.

YOU'RE GLAD THEY FIXED THE ARM PLACEMENT
AFTER THE STATUE OF GLOOSCAP WAS "ERECTED."

YOU NEVER FORGOT THE DAY YOU DISCOVERED CRYSTAL CRESCENT HAD A THIRD BEACH.

YOU REMEMBER WHEN YOU HAD YOUR OWN SCHOOL UNIFORM.

YOU CAN SPOT PEOPLE FROM THE PROVINCE BY THEIR CARRY-ON LUGGAGE.

YOU DEEP-FRY PEPPERONI.

YOU KNOW BETTER THAN TO EAT YELLOW SNOW,
BUT YOU CAN'T GET ENOUGH BROWN SNOW.

THE FIRST "I" IN "IMAGINE" IS SILENT.

THE "U" IS SILENT IN "AUNT."

YOU KNOW WHERE THE NOVA SCOTIANS LIVE.

YOUR LIVERPOOL MUSIC MUSEUM HAS NOTHING TO DO WITH THE BEATLES.

YOU CAN'T TELL THE DIFFERENCE BETWEEN A BAGPIPE PLAYED BY A PROFESSIONAL AND A BAGPIPE PLAYED BY AN AMATEUR.

YOU REMEMBER WHEN THE TRAILER PARK BOYS MADE RITA MACNEIL HARVEST MARIJUANA AT GUNPOINT.

YOUR BIRTHDAY CAKE HAS MORE ICING THAN CAKE.

YOU CALL LUSKINIKN "FOUR CENTS" BECAUSE AT ONE TIME THE INGREDIENTS COST FOUR CENTS.

THIS IS NO CONTEST.

THERE WAS A HUGE DIFFERENCE BETWEEN WHAT YOU ORDERED AND WHAT YOU GOT.

IT SEEMED LIKE THERE WAS ALWAYS SOMEBODY HOSING DOWN THE ZIPPER.

EVEN THOUGH THE HALFWAY MARK BETWEEN THE EQUATOR AND THE NORTH POLE CIRCLES THE EARTH, IN NOVA SCOTIA IT ONLY EXISTS IN STEWIACKE.

YOU GAVE THE RIGHT-OF-WAY TO A RIGHT WHALE.

YOU WENT WHALE WATCHING IN YOUR CAR.

THIS IS HOW YOU WATERPROOF YOUR BOOTS.

YOU KNOW TWO CELEBRITIES NAMED COOKIE.

YOU'RE PROUD THAT THE FIRST ALL-BLACK BATTALION IN CANADA DURING WWI WAS FORMED IN NOVA SCOTIA.

YOU LANDED ON THE BEACHES OF NORMANDY.

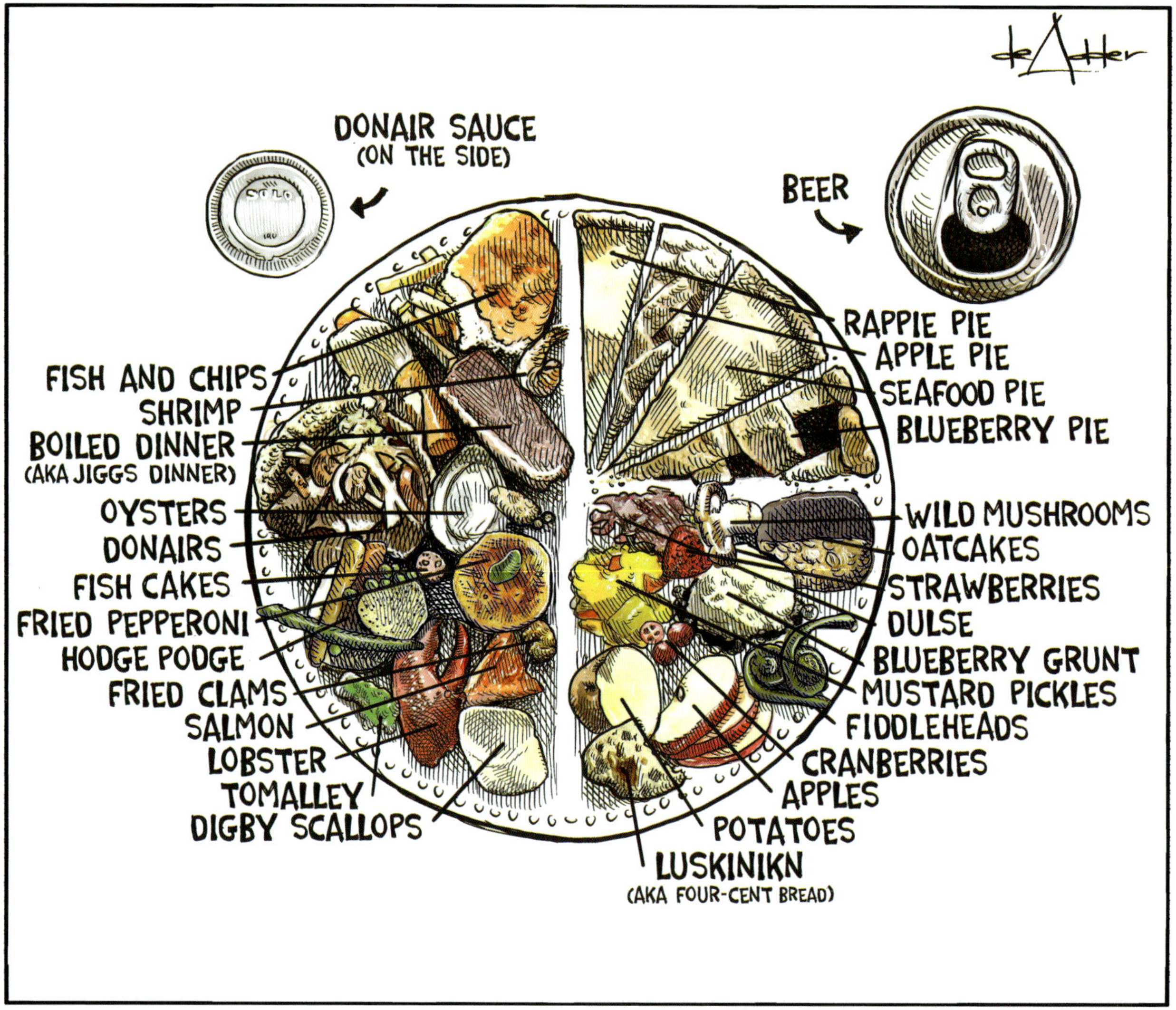

THIS IS YOUR FOOD GUIDE.

YOUR FAVOURITE COOK BOOK HAS SEEN BETTER DAYS.

THIS IS YOUR SIDNEY CROSBY ROOKIE CARD.

YOU REMEMBER GETTING YOUR FIRST NEW $10 BILL.

YOU'VE HAD A BEACH ALL TO YOURSELF.

THE TOP NEWS STORY OF THE DAY IS LOBSTERS BEING STOLEN.

YOU WENT FISHING AND ALL YOU CAUGHT WAS A BUZZ.

YOU START TO DREAD THE RETURN OF
WINTER AND IT'S ONLY AUGUST.

YOU WERE WARNED TO BE PREPARED.

YOU ASKED A FISHERMAN IF HE HAS CRABS.

YOU'VE BEEN TO YOUR FAIR SHARE OF REGATTAS.

YOU'VE BEEN TO YOUR FAIR SHARE OF FESTIVALS.

YOU BOUGHT ICE CREAM IN A SNOW STORM.

THE WETTEST YOU EVER FELT WAS AT STANFEST.

THERE ARE A MULTITUDE OF STRANGE WAYS TO GET AROUND BUT UBER ISN'T ONE.

YOU THINK THIS WHOLE PROVINCE IS A BIT OBSESSED.

THE BIRTHPLACE OF HOCKEY IS NOT UP FOR DEBATE.

YOU THINK EVERYBODY GOT THE MEMO
ON HOW TO DRESS IN THE MORNING.

YOU REMEMBER KILLER KARL KRUPP, SWEET DADDY SIKI
AND THE CUBAN ASSASSIN.

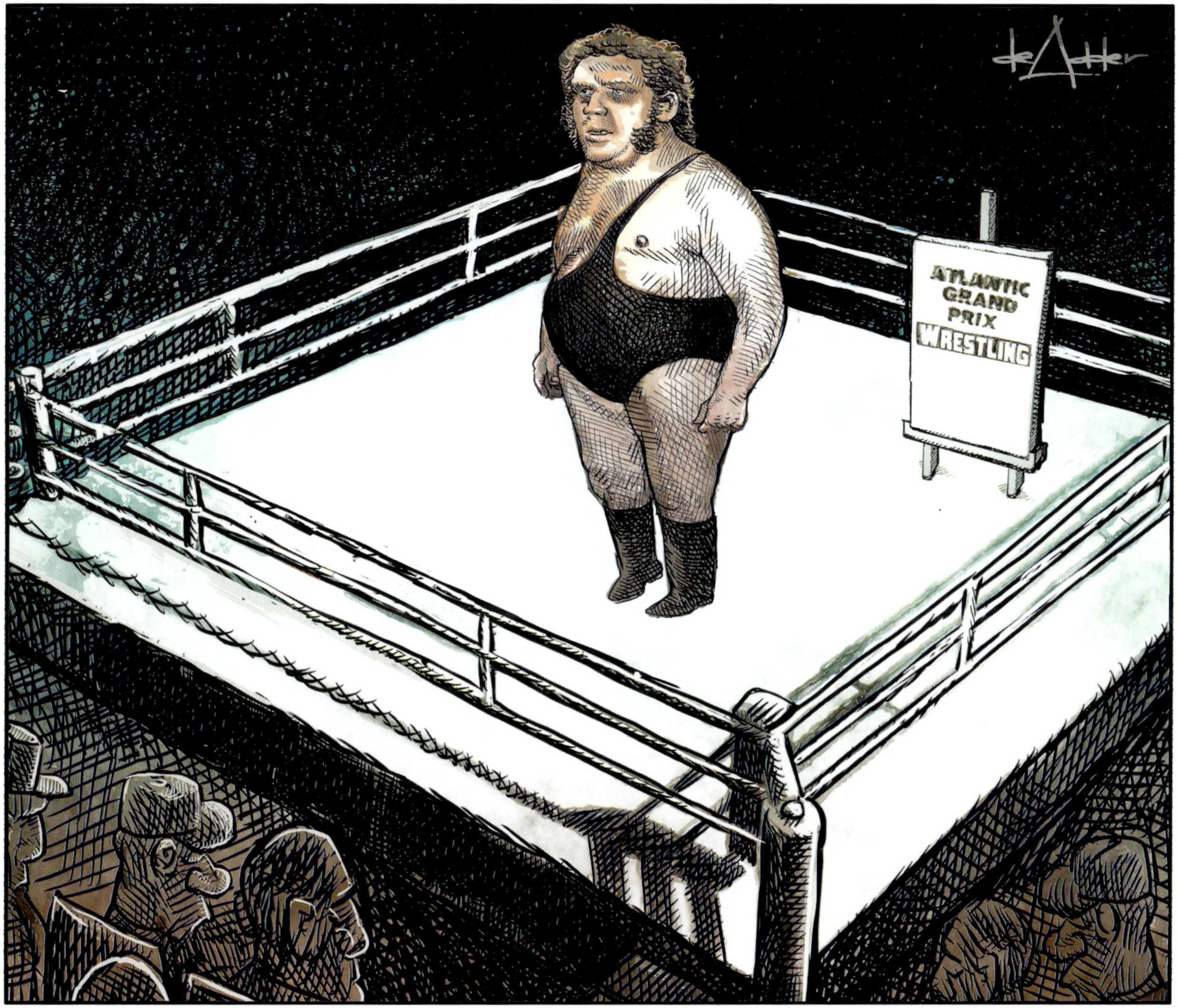

YOU KNEW ANDRE THE GIANT BEFORE HE HIT THE BIG TIME.

YOU KNOW NOVA SCOTIA HAS SOME OF THE BIGGEST ATTRACTIONS.

YOU KNOW NOVA SCOTIA HAS SOME OF THE SMALLEST ATTRACTIONS.

YOU VAGUELY REMEMBER GOING TO PIZZA CORNER LAST NIGHT.

WHERE TO GET THE BEST FISH AND CHIPS CAN LEAD TO A HEATED ARGUMENT.

YOU'VE DRUNK DIALED FROM A PHONE BOOTH IN THE MIDDLE OF A FIELD.

YOUR FAVOURITE SHIRT IS FROM FRENCHY'S.

YOUR NOVA SCOTIA DUCK TOLLING RETRIEVER
NEVER GETS TIRED OF RETRIEVING.

YOU DIDN'T HAVE A GOLDEN GLOW THE NEXT MORNING.

YOU KNOW JOHN CABOT DIDN'T "DISCOVER" ANYTHING.

IN CASE OF ZOMBIE APOCALYPSE, YOU HAVE A SHORT DRIVE TO FREEPORT, NS.

SHAG HARBOUR IS YOUR AREA 51.

YOU WALKED ON THE OCEAN'S FLOOR.

YOU KNOW APRIL SHOWERS BRING MAY FLOWERS, BUT JUNE BRINGS JUNE BUGS.

THE REST OF THE SUMMER IS TICK SEASON.

YOU THINK A BOOK ON OUTHOUSES IS A GREAT COFFEE TABLE BOOK.

YOU DON'T BELIEVE THE EASTERN COUGAR IS EXTINCT.

WHEN SOMEBODY FROM AWAY SAYS THEY ARE COMING FOR A VISIT, YOU INSIST THEY TIME IT DURING THE SUMMER MONTHS

YOU CHEERED FOR A TEAM OF MILLIONAIRES, 59 YEARS BEFORE THE FIRST NHL STAR BECAME A MILLIONAIRE.

YOU GREW UP IN THE LARGEST BLACK COMMUNITY IN CANADA.

THE FIRST TIME YOU SAW THE TRAGICALLY HIP WAS AT THE MISTY MOON, THE LAST TIME WAS AT THE GRAND PARADE.

MARIJUANA ISN'T THE ONLY EDIBLE WEED.

YOU'RE AS STUNNED AS SOMEONE'S ARSE.

YOU FELT LIKE YOU WERE IN CHILDREN OF THE CORN.

THERE'S LOTS OF PIZZA LEFT BECAUSE EVERYBODY FILLED UP ON THE GARLIC FINGERS.

YOU REMEMBER WHEN BEEP WAS DELIVERED TO YOUR DOOR.

YOU WERE CONVINCED THAT YOU WERE A CHICKEN.

SHUBENACADIE SAM SAW HIS SHADOW.

FEBRUARY IS THE LONGEST MONTH.

YOU'VE FOUND A 300-MILLION YEAR OLD FOSSIL ON THE BEACH.

YOU TRIED TO MAKE THE GUARD AT CITADEL HILL SMILE.

YOU PARKED A HALF MILE AWAY TO CHASE THE ACE.

YOU REMEMBER WHEN PEOPLE WENT TO OXFORD TO TAKE A SELFIE WITH A BLUEBERRY.

NO MATTER WHERE YOU ARE IN NOVA SCOTIA,
THE OCEAN ISN'T FAR AWAY.

YOUR FAMILY VACATION WAS IN MONCTON.

YOU LIVE ON GLOOSCAP'S BED.

YOU HELD A LOBSTER RACE WHERE THE WINNER GOT BOILED ALIVE.

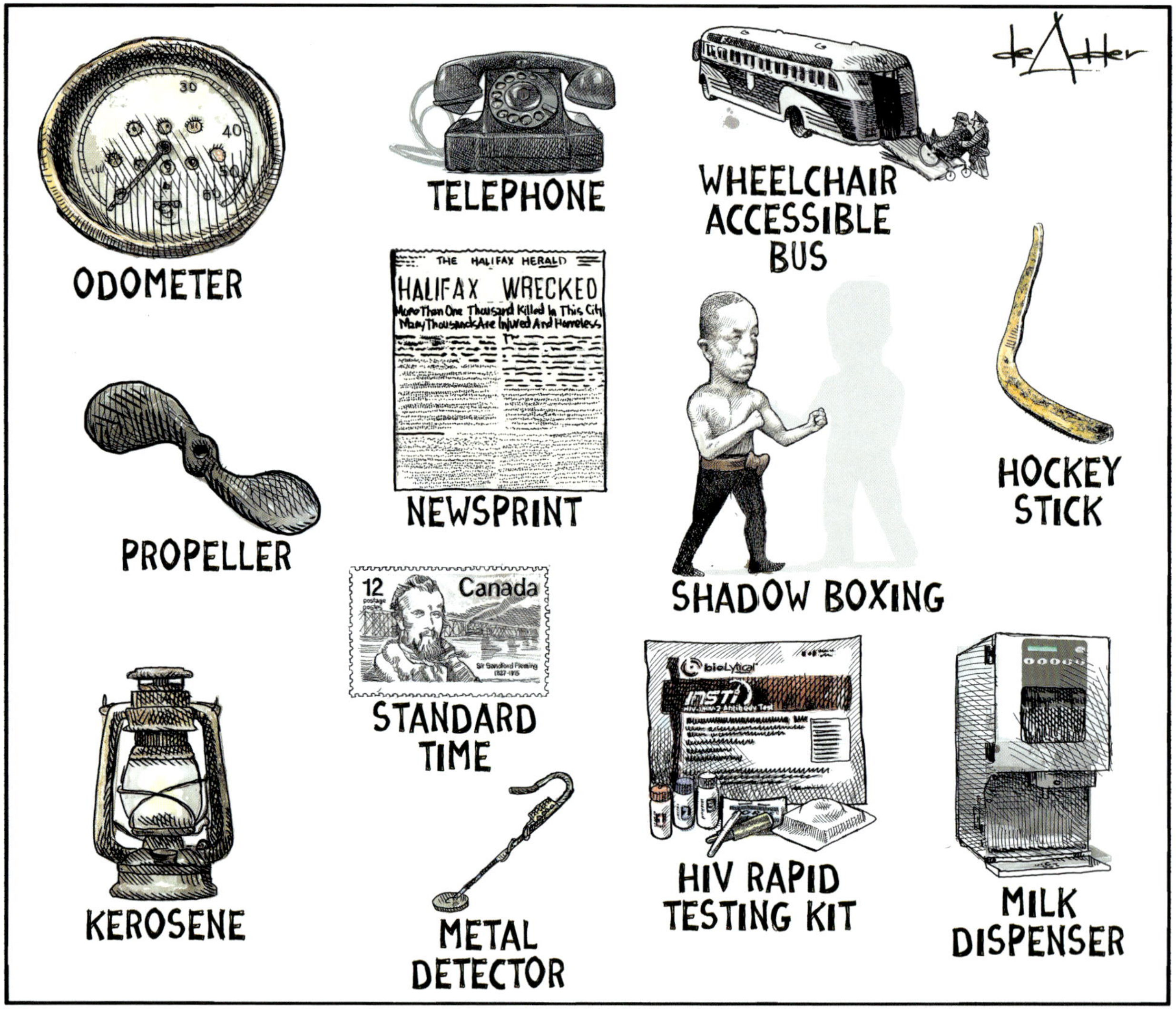

YOUR INVENTIONS CHANGED THE WORLD.

YOU KNOW TWO OF THE BEST BOXERS
IN HISTORY ARE FROM NOVA SCOTIA.

YOU GOT STUCK BEHIND A STEEL POST AT THE FORUM.

YOU'VE GOTTEN TEARY-EYED WATCHING A MEN'S CHOIR SING.

YOU STILL HAVE A NOVA SCOTIA VOYAGEURS JERSEY.

YOU GREW UP READING BOB CHAMBERS.

YOU STOOD FOR O CANADA IN MI'KMAQ.

YOUR PROTESTS ARE SMALL BUT MIGHTY.

YOU'VE HAD A HUNCH PEOPLE WERE LAUGHING AT YOU.

YOU MISS THE BEER WARS.

A TATTOO ISN'T SOMETHING YOU HAVE REMOVED WHEN YOU TURN 40.

YOU WERE BLOWN OVER BY LES SUÊTES.

YOU THINK DONAIRS SHOULD ALSO HAVE THEIR OWN BIBS.

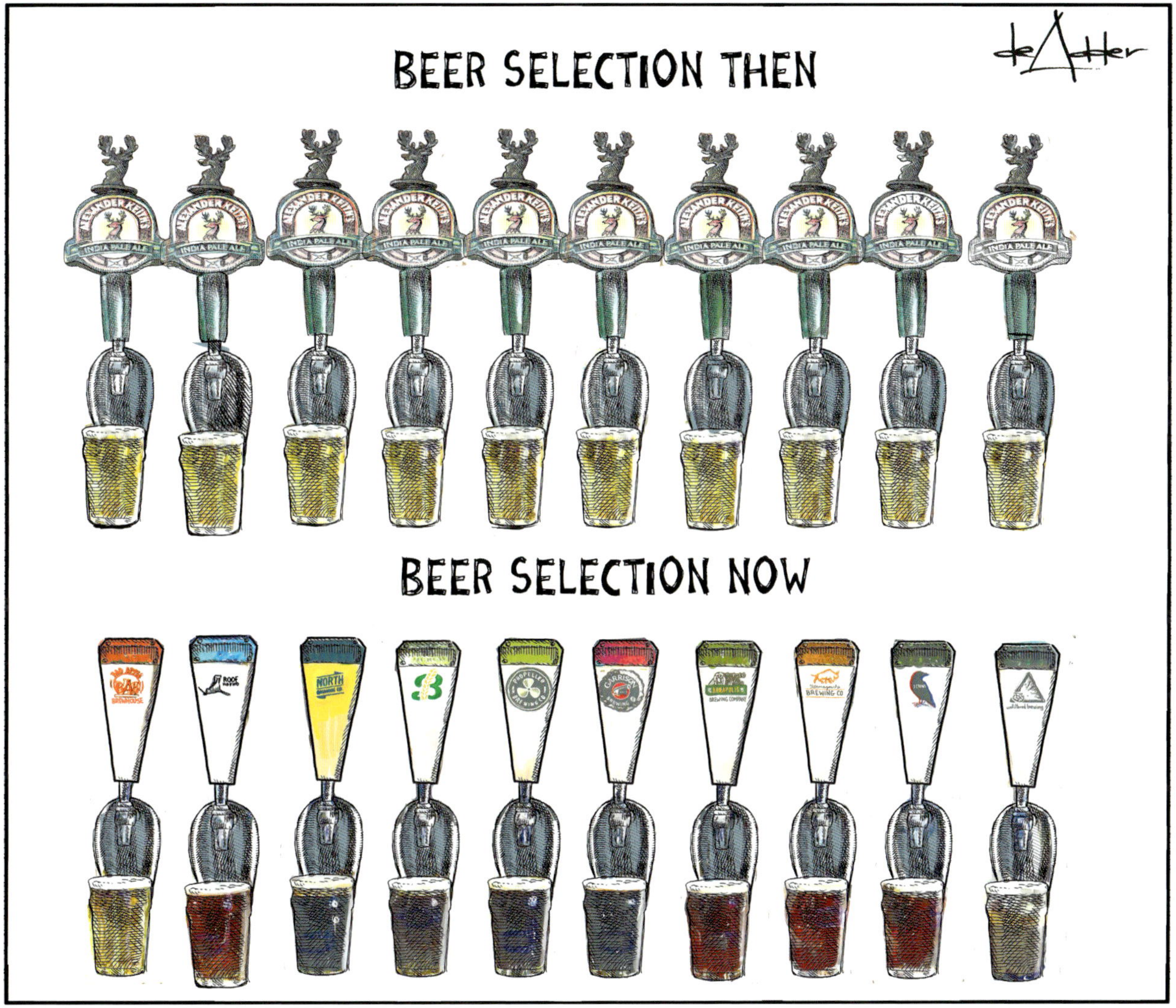

YOU NEED A FIELD GUIDE JUST TO ORDER A LOCAL BEER.

THE WORD "ARSE" IS VERSATILE.

EVERY TIME YOU WENT TO SHUBENACADIE WILDLIFE PARK
IT WAS THE ANIMALS' NAP TIME.

YOU DON'T HAVE A FAMILY DOCTOR.

YOU'VE LIVED IN ANOTHER PROVINCE FOR YEARS, BUT STILL CALL NOVA SCOTIA HOME.

END NOTES FOR COME-FROM-AWAYS

Page 7 — Nova Scotians united in a show of grief by leaving seven stuffed animals on doorsteps and windowsills in honour of the seven children from the Barho family who perished in a tragic 2019 Halifax house fire. News of these acts spread quickly and #Bears4BarhoChildren became a worldwide outpouring of support.

Page 8 — When water vapour remains in the air as humidity, it makes the air feel warmer.

Page 9 — If rocks appear black, it means that they are wet and that you are too close to the surf. Strong waves can pull you into the ocean.

Page 10 — Caribou, Nova Scotia (NS).

Page 11 — Nova Scotians who fly in winter know that weather conditions can ground flights, sometimes for days, shortening their escape.

Page 12 — Cobequid Pass.

Page 13 — Of course, those signs only apply during the winter months, but they remain in place all year long.

Page 14 — Nathan MacKinnon is from Springhill, Sidney Crosby is from Cole Harbour, and Brad Marchand is from Hammonds Plains.

Page 15 — Al MacInnis is one of the best defencemen that ever played in the National Hockey League (NHL).

Page 16 — *Boughten bread* is bread that was purchased, not home-baked.

Page 17 — Brown bread is not whole wheat bread. It is bread made with molasses.

Page 18 and 19 — On September 29th, 2003, Hurricane Juan made landfall in Nova Scotia as a Category 2 hurricane.

Page 20 and 21 — Power regularly goes out in Halifax.

Page 22 and 23 — The original Dartmouth IKEA, which opened in 1975, was the first IKEA store in North America. It closed in the late 1980s due to falling sales. IKEA returned to Halifax/Dartmouth in 2018.

Page 24 — Christmas trees, blueberries, apples, and seafood are four of Nova Scotia's biggest exports.

Page 25 — Brothers Meats in Halifax makes the best pepperoni in the world. The donair was invented here. Stanfield's underwear is based in Truro. Pictou County residents believe that Pictou County has the best pizza in the world. Mabou is a hotbed of musical talent. Sydney has the world's largest statue of a fiddle.

Page 26 — Nova Scotians, for the most part, refuse to pay the high price of lobster in a restaurant.

Page 27 — Nova Scotians have their ways of getting lobster for much less than they would pay in a store or restaurant.

Page 28 — The word *sook* is used like the word "sulk" in the rest of the world. As in *sooky baby*.

Page 29 — *Puck* means "to punch."

Page 30 — When the giant statue of Glooscap was first erected near Truro, the arm placement was anatomically suggestive. It was later adjusted.

Page 31 — Crystal Crescent's 3rd beach is a nude beach.

Page 32 — If you grew up in the 70s and 80s, hunting jackets were in style or, at least, were widely worn. They became a symbol of non-conformity.

Page 33 — Sobeys bags are so prevalent in the province that many Nova Scotians call all plastic shopping bags "Sobeys bags."

Page 34 — Fried pepperoni is a *thing* in Nova Scotia — mostly because of Brothers pepperoni.

Page 35 — When maple syrup is boiled and spread on snow, it becomes maple candy.

Page 36 and 37 — Nova Scotians have many words they pronounce in their own, unique way.

Page 38 — Nova Scotian pride can be seen around the world, as young Nova Scotians often use flags as curtains.

Page 39 — Hank Snow was born in Nova Scotia. There is a museum dedicated to his life and music in Liverpool, NS.

Page 40 — Bagpipes are frequently heard in Nova Scotia at a variety of functions. Nova Scotia isn't called New Scotland fer nuttin!

Page 41 — This cartoon is in reference to an episode of one of Nova Scotia's most popular exports, the *Trailer Park Boys*.

Page 42 — Boiled icing chocolate cake is a staple at Nova Scotian birthdays.

Page 43 — Mi'kmaq bread is called *luskinikn* (pronounced loo-skin-e-gen).

Page 44 — Pictou County claims to have the best pizza in the world.

Page 45 — The McLobster is a seasonal treat that is offered only in Atlantic Canada and Maine. Recent high prices for lobster have caused it to be taken off the menu.

Page 46 — The Bill Lynch Show is a travelling carnival that moves from town to town. It seemed that every night somebody had too much to eat before going on the Zipper.

Page 47 — Stewiacke, NS.

Page 48 — Right whales are nearly extinct. Seasonal restrictions have been put in place for ocean-going vessels, in an effort to cut down on collisions and save the few remaining whales.

Page 49 — It's not uncommon to see whales from the coast. You have to be in the right place at the right time, though.

Page 50 — Putting plastic bread bags inside boots is an effective way to keep your feet dry.

Page 51 — Cookie Rankin is a member of Nova Scotia's first family of music — the Rankins. Cookie Monster is a monster who likes cookies.

Page 52 — The No. 2 Construction Battalion was authorized on July 5th, 1916, during the First World War. It was the first and only all-Black battalion in Canadian history.

Page 53 — The men of the North Nova Scotia Highlanders infantry regiment landed at Juno Beach on D-Day, June 6th, 1944, many carrying bicycles. These bicycles proved useless in practice and soldiers abandoned them soon after the landing.

Page 54 and 55 — Nova Scotians have their own, unique dishes and ways of cooking.

Page 56 — Sidney Crosby was born in Cole Harbour. Many Nova Scotians knew that he was a special hockey player, even at an early age.

Page 57 — Viola Desmond, as of the publishing of this book, is the latest person to appear on Canada's money. Born in Halifax, she is widely known as the Rosa Parks of Canada for her refusal to leave the whites-only area of the Roseland Theatre in New Glasgow, NS. But Nova Scotians call Rosa Parks the Viola Desmond of America, as Desmond's story came before Parks' story.

Page 58 — There are so many beaches in Nova Scotia that it is not uncommon to find you have the beach to yourself.

Page 59 — It seems like every year somebody steals a catch of lobster and the RCMP have to investigate.

Page 62 — Frankie MacDonald of Whitney Pier made a name for himself with his YouTube weather forecasts and reports about weather phenomena. To date, his videos have received over 32 million views. As Frankie says, “Be prepared!”

Page 67 — Stan Rogers Folk Festival, Canso, NS.

Page 70 — Other places in Canada and across the world falsely claim to be the birthplace of hockey, but Nova Scotians know it’s Windsor, NS.

Page 71 — While attending Acadia University, Alex MacLean started East Coast Lifestyle as a class project. Today it’s impossible to go anywhere in Nova Scotia without seeing somebody wearing one of his hoodies or t-shirts.

Page 72 and 73 — Before World Wrestling Entertainment (WWE) there was Atlantic Grand Prix Wrestling, a wrestling entertainment troupe that travelled from town to town across Atlantic Canada.

Page 76 — Pizza Corner is a popular area of the Halifax downtown that at one time had three pizza joints. On the weekends and after the bars closed, it was *the* place to go for a late-night snack. Today it’s down to one pizza shop, but it’s still called Pizza Corner.

Page 78 — Annapolis Valley is the wine region of Nova Scotia and is known for white and ice wines. Luckett Vineyards has a working British phone booth.

Page 79 — Frenchy’s is a well-known used clothing chain.

Page 80 — The Nova Scotia Duck Tolling Retriever is the provincial dog of Nova Scotia.

Page 82 — It’s inaccurate to say John Cabot discovered a place that was already inhabited.

Page 83 — At the end of the movie *World War Z* starring Brad Pitt, everyone takes refuge in the last safe place in North America — Freeport, NS.

Page 84 — Shag Harbour is the site of a famous 1967 Unidentified Flying Object (UFO) incident.

Page 85 — In some places on the coast in the Bay of Fundy the tide goes out so far you can literally walk on the bottom of the ocean.

Page 89 — Most scientists claim the eastern cougar to be extinct. But many sightings have been reported by people walking in Nova Scotia’s backcountry, including one by the author of this book. I swear I saw something that looked like a cougar.

Page 90 — Nova Scotia is always beautiful, but during the summer, it is paradise!

Page 91 — The Sydney Millionaires were a professional hockey team from Cape Breton that made it all the way to the Stanley Cup finals in 1913.

Page 94 — Fiddleheads are the furled fronds of a young fern. They are considered a delicacy and are only available for a few weeks in the spring. They are eaten as a vegetable side dish.

Page 95 — “You’re as stunned as me arse” is a common insult in Nova Scotia.

Page 96 — Noggins Corner Farm Market, Greenwich, NS.

Page 97 — Garlic fingers are an Atlantic Canadian food served with donair sauce.

Page 98 — Beep was a fruit juice drink made by Farmers Co-operative Dairy.

Page 99 — Reveen was an illusionist and hypnotist who often toured in Atlantic Canada.

Page 102 — The Joggins Fossil Cliffs — a UNESCO World Heritage Site — have exposed layers of rock which show the most complete fossil record of life during the Coal Age.

Page 104 — Chase the Ace is a form of lottery that has taken Nova Scotia by storm.

Page 105 — A sinkhole opened up in Oxford in 2018 and quickly grew, swallowing up trees, picnic tables, and part of a parking lot near the Oxford Lions Club.

Page 108 — Glooscap is a legendary figure of the Mi'kmaq people. In his role as Creator, he formed many of the geographical features of Atlantic Canada, including mountains, hills, and lakes. Nova Scotia is considered to be his bed, while neighbouring Prince Edward Island is considered his pillow.

Page 111 — George Dixon has been ranked by some as the #1 Featherweight boxer of all time. Sam Langford was known as the "Greatest Fighter Nobody Knows," and some boxing historians consider him the greatest fighter of all time.

Page 113 — The Men of the Deeps is North America's only coal miners chorus.

Page 114 — The Nova Scotia Voyageurs was a Halifax-based American Hockey League (AHL) team and were the affiliate team of the Montreal Canadiens.

Page 115 — Bob Chambers was the editorial cartoonist for the Halifax *Chronicle Herald* newspaper. He had a celebrated career that lasted 53 years.

Page 116 — The Mi'kmaq version of *O Canada* is performed or played regularly at functions in Nova Scotia. Many schools play it during Mi'kmaq History Month in October.

Page 117 — To coincide with the epic Women's March on Washington in 2017, a small group of women held their own march in Sandy Cove, NS. News of their march went viral on the internet and was carried by news outlets around the world.

Page 119 — The so-called *draft wars* took place in the late 80s and early 90s when alcohol prices were unregulated. The lack of regulation led to bars undercutting each other's prices in an effort to attract customers.

Page 120 — The Royal Nova Scotia International Tattoo is an annual show in Halifax which features military bands and display teams.

Page 121 — *Les Suêtes* are strong south-east winds that occur on the west coast of Cape Breton Island.